A CENTURY *of*
LEWISHAM

It was not much to declare in 1901 that Horniman's Museum was the finest building completed in Lewisham during the twentieth century. Today, alas, the same compliment can be paid with greater effect. Harrison Townsend's masterpiece was begun in the nineteenth century in Camberwell and may still have been there when this photograph of the building work was taken. Lewisham captured the prize after a boundary adjustment in 1900.

A CENTURY of LEWISHAM

JOHN COULTER

SUTTON PUBLISHING

This book was first published in 1999 by Sutton Publishing Limited.

This new paperback edition first published in 2007 by
Sutton Publishing, an imprint of NPI Media Group
Cirencester Road · Chalford · Stroud · Gloucestershire · GL6 8PE

British Library Cataloguing in Publication Data
A catalogue record for this book is available from the British Library.

ISBN 978-0-7509-4935-4

Front endpaper: Large crowds gathered in Ladywell Road to greet the Prince and Princess of Wales when
they opened the St Olave's workhouse, later Ladywell Lodge, on 12 July 1900.
Back endpaper: The new Lewisham transport system taking shape in July 1999, with the Docklands Light
Railway station (centre) nearing completion.
Half title page: Jack Rags was the nickname of Frederick Mark Burton, a celebrated Lewisham tramp in the
early years of the century. He died in 1917.
Title page: Helen Ann Attridge, a maid employed in Jerningham Road, New Cross, in 1900.

Typeset in Photina.
Typesetting and origination by
Sutton Publishing.
Printed and bound in England.

Contents

The old Sayes Court workhouse at Deptford had a varied career after the paupers were removed in the late 1830s. By 1900, when this inmate was photographed, the building was being used as almshouses for aged tenants of the Evelyn estate.

Britain: A Century
of Change

Children gathered around an early wireless set in the 1920s. The speed
and forms of communication were to change dramatically as the century
advanced. (*Barnaby's Picture Library*)

The delirious rejoicing at the news of the Relief of Mafeking, during the Boer War in May 1900, is a colourful historical moment. But, in retrospect, the introduction that year of the first motor bus was rather more important, signalling another major adjustment to town life. In the previous 60 years railway stations, post-and-telegraph offices, police and fire stations, gas works and gasometers, new livestock markets and covered markets, schools, churches, football grounds, hospitals and asylums, water pumping stations and sewerage plants had totally altered the urban scene, as the country's population tripled and over 70 per cent were born in or moved to the towns.

When Queen Victoria died in 1901, she was measured for her coffin by her grandson Kaiser Wilhelm, the London prostitutes put on black mourning and the blinds came down in the villas and terraces spreading out from the old town centres. These centres were reachable by train and tram, by the new bicycles and still newer motor cars, connected by the new telephone, and lit by gas or even electricity. The shops may have been full of British-made cotton and woollen clothing but the grocers and butchers were selling cheap Danish bacon, Argentinian beef, Australasian mutton, tinned or dried fish and fruit from Canada, California and South Africa. Most of these goods were carried in British-built-and-crewed ships, burning Welsh steam coal.

Women working as porters on the Great Western Railway, Paddington, *c. 1917. (W.L. Kenning/ Adrian Vaughan Collection)*

As the first decade moved on, the Open Spaces Act meant more parks, bowling greens and cricket pitches. The first state pensions came in, together with higher taxation and death duties. These were raised mostly to pay for the new Dreadnought battleships needed to maintain naval superiority over Germany, and deter them from war. But the deterrent did not work. The First World War transformed the place of women, as they took over many men's jobs. Its other legacies were the war memorials which joined the statues of Victorian worthies in main squares round the land. After 1918 death duties bit even harder and a quarter of England changed hands in a few years.

The multiple shop – the chain store – appeared in the high street: Sainsburys, Maypole, Lipton's, Home & Colonial, the Fifty Shilling Tailor, Burton, Boots, W.H. Smith. The shopper was spoilt for choice, attracted by the brash fascias and advertising hoardings for national brands like Bovril, Pears Soap, and Ovaltine. Many new buildings began to be seen, such as garages, motor showrooms, picture palaces (cinemas), 'palais de dance', and the bow-windowed, pebble-dashed, tile-hung, half-timbered houses that were built as ribbon-development along the roads and new bypasses or on the new estates nudging the green belts.

During the 1920s cars became more reliable and sophisticated as well as commonplace, with developments like the electric self-starter making them easier for women to drive. Who wanted to turn a crank handle in the new short skirt? This was, indeed, the electric age as much as the motor era. Trolley buses, electric trams and trains extended mass transport and electric light replaced gas in the street and the home, which itself was groomed by the vacuum cleaner.

A major jolt to the march onward and upward was administered by the Great Depression of the early 1930s. The older British industries – textiles, shipbuilding, iron, steel, coal – were already under pressure from foreign competition when this worldwide slump arrived, cutting exports by half in two years and producing 3 million unemployed (and still rising) by 1932. Luckily there were new diversions to alleviate the misery. The 'talkies' arrived in the cinemas; more and more radios and gramophones were to be found in people's homes; there were new women's magazines, with fashion, cookery tips and problem pages; football pools; the flying feats of women pilots like Amy Johnson; the Loch Ness Monster; cheap chocolate and the drama of Edward VIII's abdication.

Father and child cycling past Buckingham Palace on VE Day, 8 May 1945. (*Hulton Getty Picture Collection*)

Things were looking up again by 1936 and unemployment was down to 2 million. New light industry was booming in the Home Counties as factories struggled to keep up with the demand for radios, radiograms, cars and electronic goods including the first television sets. The threat from Hitler's Germany meant rearmament, particularly of the airforce, which stimulated aircraft and aero engine firms. If you were lucky and lived in the south, there was good money to be earned. A semi-detached house cost £450, a Morris Cowley £150. People may have smoked like chimneys but life expectancy, since 1918, was up by 15 years while the birth rate had almost halved. The fifty-four hour week was down to forty-eight hours and there were 9 million radio licences by 1939.

In some ways it is the little memories that seem to linger longest from the Second World War: the kerbs painted white to show up in the

A family gathered
around their
television set in
the 1950s. (*Hulton
Getty Picture
Collection*)

blackout, the rattle of ack-ack shrapnel on roof tiles, sparrows killed by
bomb blast, painting your legs brown and then adding a black seam
down the back to simulate stockings. The biggest damage, apart from
London, was in the south-west (Plymouth, Bristol) and the Midlands
(Coventry, Birmingham). Postwar reconstruction was rooted in the
Beveridge Report which set out the expectations for the Welfare State.
This, together with the nationalisation of the Bank of England, coal,
gas, electricity and the railways, formed the programme of the Labour
government in 1945. At this time the USA was calling in its debts and
Britain was beggared by the war, yet still administering its Empire.

Times were hard in the late 1940s, with rationing even more stringent
than during the war. Yet this was, as has been said, 'an innocent and
well-behaved era'. The first let-up came in 1951 with the Festival of
Britain and then there was another fillip in 1953 from the Coronation,

which incidentally gave a huge boost to the spread of TV. By 1954 leisure motoring had been resumed but the Comet – Britain's best hope for taking on the American aviation industry – suffered a series of mysterious crashes. The Suez debacle of 1956 was followed by an acceleration in the withdrawal from Empire, which had begun in 1947 with the Independence of India. Consumerism was truly born with the advent of commercial TV and most homes soon boasted washing machines, fridges, electric irons and fires.

The *Lady Chatterley* obscenity trial in 1960 was something of a straw in the wind for what was to follow in that decade. A collective loss of inhibition seemed to sweep the land, as stately home owners opened up, the Beatles and the Rolling Stones transformed popular music, and retailing, cinema and the theatre were revolutionised. Designers, hairdressers, photographers and models moved into places vacated by an Establishment put to flight by the new breed of satirists spawned by *Beyond the Fringe* and *Private Eye*.

In the 1970s Britain seems to have suffered a prolonged hangover after the excesses of the previous decade. Ulster, inflation and union troubles were not made up for by entry into the EEC, North Sea Oil, Women's Lib or, indeed, Punk Rock. Mrs Thatcher applied the corrective in the 1980s, as the country moved more and more from its old manufacturing base over to providing services, consulting, advertising, and expertise in the 'invisible' market of high finance or in IT. Britain entertained the world with *Cats*, *Phantom of the Opera*, *Four Weddings and a Funeral*, *The Full Monty*, *Mr Bean* and the *Teletubbies*.

The post-1945 townscape has seen changes to match those in the worlds of work, entertainment and politics. In 1956 the Clean Air Act served notice on smogs and pea-souper fogs, smuts and blackened buildings, forcing people to stop burning coal and go over to smokeless sources of heat and energy. In the same decade some of the best urban building took place in the 'new towns' like Basildon, Crawley, Stevenage and Harlow. Elsewhere open warfare was declared on slums and what was labelled inadequate, cramped, back-to-back, two-up, two-down, housing. The new 'machine for living in' was a flat in a high-rise block. The architects and planners who promoted these were in league with the traffic engineers, determined to keep the motor car moving whatever the price in multi-storey car parks, meters, traffic wardens and ring roads.

Carnaby Street in the 1960s. (*Barnaby's Picture Library*)

11

The Millennium Dome at Greenwich, 1999. (*Michael Durnan/Barnaby's Picture Library*)

The old pollutant, coal smoke, was replaced by petrol and diesel exhaust, and traffic noise. Even in the back garden it was hard to find peace as motor mowers, then leaf blowers and strimmers made themselves heard, and the neighbours let you share their choice of music from their powerful new amplifiers, whether you wanted to or not. Fast food was no longer only a pork pie in a pub or fish-and-chips. There were Indian curry houses, Chinese take-aways and American-style hamburgers, while the drinker could get away from beer in a wine bar. Under the impact of television the big Gaumonts and Odeons closed or were rebuilt as multi-screen cinemas, while the palais de dance gave way to discos and clubs.

From the late 1960s the introduction of listed buildings and conservation areas, together with the growth of preservation societies, put a brake on 'comprehensive redevelopment'. Now the new risk at the end of the 1990s is that town centres may die, as shoppers are attracted to the edge-of-town supermarkets surrounded by parking space, where much more than food and groceries can be bought. The ease of the one-stop shop represents the latest challenge to the good health of our towns. But with care, ingenuity and a determination to keep control of our environment, this challenge can be met.

Lewisham: An Introduction

If it were possible to find objective accounts of Lewisham in 1900 and in 1999, and to print them with the names suppressed, no reader would believe that they described the same place. Physically, morally, politically, religiously, economically, racially, even geographically, the suburbs that make up the modern borough have lost touch with the ancient parishes from which they emerged a century ago. There is hardly any continuity of blood, for it is a rarity to find a current Lewisham family that was established in the district before 1900. A picture book is not the place to enter into a serious discussion of the causes of these profound changes, but perhaps this loose chronicle can provide some anecdotal indication of the stages by which the modern town has emerged from the old villages.

The London Borough of Lewisham is a combination of three old Kentish parishes, St Margaret Lee, St Mary Lewisham, and St Paul

The Old House at Sydenham, formerly the home of the Mayow family, shortly before it was demolished in 1902. The Grand Parade in Sydenham Road and the Thorpe Estate were built on the site of the house and its garden.

Deptford. Lee and Lewisham, which had a similar history as farming communities turning gradually into commuter suburbs, were brought together painlessly in 1900 to form the Metropolitan Borough of Lewisham. St Paul Deptford, which was carved out of the ancient parish of St Nicholas in 1730, and became a Metropolitan Borough in 1900, was a very different place.

The working Deptford Creek at the beginning of the twentieth century. The view is towards the Ravensbourne Wharf on the right bank of the river, just south of Creek Bridge.

In the eighteenth and nineteenth centuries Lewisham and Lee had been the home of many merchants, bankers, lawyers, government officials and others wealthy enough to commute to town in private carriages or the expensive public coaches. A wider range of middle class residents settled in the 1850s and '60s, when the railways made travel somewhat cheaper, but it was not until the 1880s and '90s, with the arrival of the trams, and the consequent reduction of railway fares, that Lewisham attracted a population of working class commuters. The wealthy families moved further into the country, and their villas were replaced by streets of terraces and semi-detached houses. By 1900 landed proprietors had practically vanished from Lewisham, and commercial clerks had become its most characteristic residents.

It was a Pooterish community, devoted to the self-help principles of former Lewisham resident Samuel Smiles. The house-proud families supported a vast array of clubs and societies to while away their leisure time in a self-improving way. Many were connected with the multitude of local churches. There were also model parliaments, discussion groups, evening classes and any number of amateur dramatic societies. The other passion of Lewisham in 1900 was sport. W.G. Grace was living in the borough, at Sydenham, county cricket was regularly played at Catford, Blackheath continued its traditional prominent role in rugby, hockey and golf, and the open spaces in the south gave ample room for dozens of sports grounds.

Deptford was a large and prosperous industrial town from the seventeenth century, when Lewisham and Lee were small farming communities, but its wealth was precarious. It depended heavily on the Royal Dockyard, which itself was at the mercy of international politics. In time of war the population was increased by workmen and their families, crowding in to earn good wages at the yard, but peace meant lay-offs, short-working, and widespread hardship. In the eighteenth century war was almost continuous, but after 1815 the

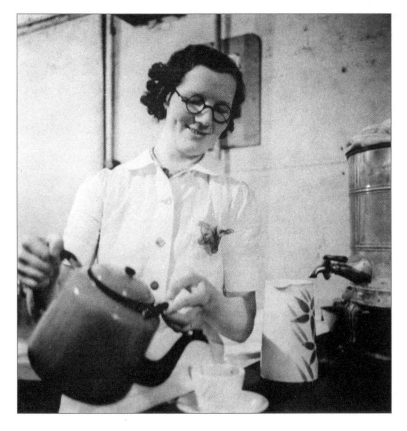

A scene in the canteen of the Woodyates Road civil defence depot near Lee Station, *c.* 1940.

general happiness of peace meant misery for Deptford. The problem was exacerbated when the growth in the size of ships meant that the Thames was no longer wide enough to launch them with safety and, one by one, throughout the nineteenth century, the private yards also closed. Heavy industry moved in to exploit cheap labour and the good transport offered by the Thames, Deptford Creek, the Surrey Canal, and the dense network of railway lines that passed through the area. But Deptford's factories did not survive the damage and disruption of the Second World War and the general trend that was taking industry

When the Labour leader Hugh Gaitskell visited Lewisham High Street on 8 April 1961, during the London County Council election campaign, a team of Conservative canvassers dogged his footsteps.

16

away from the capital. By the time Lewisham and Deptford were forced unwillingly together in 1965 as the London Borough of Lewisham, Deptford was one of the poorest areas in London.

In 1900 Deptford was almost entirely covered with buildings, streets and railway lines. Parks and playing fields were few and small, and building land practically non-existent. The council began to look beyond its own boundaries as soon as the question of providing council housing arose at the end of the First World War. In Lewisham and Lee there was still a substantial belt of farmland in the south at the beginning of the century. It did not take long for these two facts to collide in the vacant spaces of the official mind.

The Forster family, the main owners of this farmland, had made some progress in building streets of good houses in the Catford area between 1900 and 1914, and resumed this work tentatively after the war. But very soon the leaders of Deptford and other inner south London boroughs persuaded the London County Council to compulsorily purchase large tracts of Forster and Baring farmland to build its Bellingham and Downham estates. The tenants were mainly drawn from overcrowded Deptford, Bermondsey, and Rotherhithe. Lewisham had long been a promised land for ambitious families from those areas, the migration south being a visible sign that they had bettered themselves. The Corbett estate on the Catford and Hither Green borders had provided many with an opportunity to achieve this new standard of living between 1896 and 1914. Now, in the 1920s, some fifty thousand more were able to make the move, but with a much less stiff entrance examination of financial success than had formerly been required.

The Second World War was a major turning point in both parts of the future London Borough of Lewisham. In Deptford the heavy bombing speeded the flight of industry, with consequent unemployment, depopulation, and increased poverty. Lewisham had comparatively little industry to lose but the destruction of so many houses did encourage the removal of those who could afford to leave to newer, safer, and leafier suburbs further from the centre of town. Those who remained had been brought closer together by the pressures of war, and the idealistic climate of 1945 gave a new political direction to Lewisham that it has generally followed in the second half of the century.

Deptford, except for an upset in 1931, has been a Labour stronghold since 1906. Lewisham was very much a Conservative area until the Second World War and recently it has been equally firm in its support for Labour. In the intervening decades it became a crucial marginal indicator of the country's political mood and was the scene of much campaigning by the party leaders. Herbert Morrison gave up a secure seat to contest and win a Lewisham constituency in 1945. Harold Macmillan, the member for Bromley, made a number of visits, as did Hugh Gaitskell, Sir Alec Douglas Home, and Harold Wilson.

In the decades since the amalgamation of the old Lewisham and Deptford boroughs in 1965, the interest of the area, to the outsider, has been mainly in the thoroughly typical nature of its struggle with the problems of late twentieth century suburban life. How to deal with the destructive urges of the bored and ineducable portion of its youth? How to beggar its neighbour by building a bigger and better shopping centre, and a more efficiently pedestrianised High Street? How to combine various races into one community without too much violence or injustice? This last has been managed fairly well when the politicians have not interfered. Here, after all, the district has had plenty of practice, for wave after wave of immigrants have been entering throughout its history and it would be vain to seek for any aboriginal population. To speak only of comparatively recent times, Deptford and Lewisham had absorbed large numbers of Welsh, Irish, Italian, German and Jewish settlers, before the West Indian, Asian and African influx of the postwar years. Balkan refugees are the most recent addition to the list.

In the new age that is upon us, Lewisham hopes to win prosperity by a side wind from the Isle of Dogs. Much money has been spent and much of the historical shape of the town sacrificed to bring the Docklands Light Railway into Lewisham, and to welcome it with a suitably sleek and modern town centre. It resembles a brand new plastic bowl held out for good things to be poured into it. Meanwhile the fragments of the old pot are discarded. As I write, three of the borough's Victorian churches are being wholly or partially demolished and the Private Banks Sports Ground, the chief redeeming feature of Catford, has been closed after 125 years.

Edwardian Days

The Lewisham clock tower was built in 1899 in commemoration of Queen Victoria's Diamond Jubilee of 1897. The clock was officially started in February 1900 by the Earl of Dartmouth, the Lord of the Manor. This photograph was taken shortly afterwards. For the tower's more recent activity see page 118.

Is there something in the end of century atmosphere that thrusts unscrupulous adventurers to the forefront of local politics? In Lewisham the leading figure of the 1880s and '90s was Theophilus William Williams, swindler, newspaperman, embezzler, and probable suicide who is seen here in 1900. It was not until he had served for two terms as the borough's first mayor that the people of Lewisham came to their senses.

Jack in the Green, the chimney sweeps' May-day festival, was observed in Deptford until the police suppressed it, *c.* 1903. Luckily, Thankfull Sturdee recorded one of the last appearances of Fowler's troop. The Deptford Jack, in his tower of greenery, is surrounded by his traditional dancing and music-making attendants.

The Town Clerk's office at 50 Tanners Hill, formerly the headquarters of the St Paul's vestry, was a cramped and cluttered room. The building, which still survives, served as the first Deptford town hall from 1900 until 1905, when the palatial building in New Cross Road was completed. (See page 24.) The photograph was taken during those six years.

Bowls in the garden of the Lewisham Conservative Club in the High Street, *c.* 1900. The club was founded at Eagle House, Lewisham Bridge, in 1883, but moved to the former Dr Brown's house, just south of the railway bridge, in the following year. The premises were destroyed by bombing during the Second World War. Between the players and the Congregational Church spire is Brooklands House, then the Liberal Club, which survives, converted into a shop as no. 272 Lewisham High Street.

The opening of Deptford Town Hall in New Cross Road on 19 July 1905, was attended by all the local dignitaries. The mayor, who had just alighted from his carriage with the mayoress, was J. Arthur Pyne of the Lewisham Way department store (see page 67). Hurrying up on the right, raising his hat, is the photographer Thankfull Sturdee, who has contributed so many fine images to this book.

This unusually cheerful class of children was gathered at Holbeach Road School, *c.* 1905. The building was then nearly new, having been opened by the School Board for London in 1898.

Kent versus Gloucestershire at Catford Bridge, probably in 1905, though the fixture was also held here in 1909. The hosts won comfortably on both occasions. The Private Banks' Ground (now most sadly closed) was a regular county venue in the early years of the century, when Kent played here once or twice a season. The view is towards two departed Catford landmarks, the old St Laurence's church, on the right, and the old town hall.

George Chapman's shop at 34 Deptford High Street achieved an unwelcome fame in 1905 when the manager, Thomas Farrow, and his wife Ann, were murdered on the night of 26 March. There was nothing unusual about the crime itself, the panicky action of surprised burglars, but the case entered legal history when two brothers, Alfred and Albert Stratton, were convicted and hanged principally on the basis of fingerprint evidence. They were the first murderers trapped by this new forensic science.

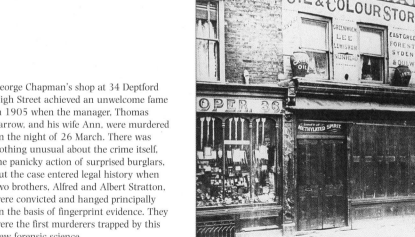

A crowded Manor House Gardens, Lee, at about the time the park was opened to the public by the London County Council in 1902. The house, once the home of the Baring family, had become a Lewisham Council library a year earlier. After our century of progress most parents are afraid to let their children play in the park.

The scene of confusion in Rushey Green during the winter of 1906–7, when the London County Council was laying tracks for its new electric trams. The view is north from the Rosenthal Road area, with the entrance to Patrol Place on the left.

After the long months of digging an excited crowd gathered at Lee Green on 25 April 1907 to see the first electric tram on the route begin its journey along Lee High Road under the watchful eye of Board of Trade inspectors. The tram is nearly hiding the New Tiger's Head. The buildings on the left, now replaced by the post office, were similar in style to the shops that survive on the other side of the pub. The terrace was continuous until the New Tiger was built.

The South Eastern, or New Cross Hospital, which had been opened in makeshift premises during the emergency of the 1877 smallpox epidemic, was rebuilt in a more solid form between 1904 and 1906. This was the nurses' sitting room when first opened.

The Quaker meeting house in Deptford High Street, which claimed Peter the Great among its former worshippers, was demolished in 1908. Thankfull Sturdee, who took the photograph, noted that the parents of Sir John Bennett, the famous watchmaker, were among those buried in the graveyard behind the meeting house.

The Park (later Hither Green) Hospital was built in 1896, in the teeth of strong local opposition, to take fever patients from all over London. Perhaps the founding of a staff football team, seen here during the 1908/9 season, helped to humanise relations with the neighbours.

An Edwards & Sons milk cart somewhere in Lee, *c.* 1909. The firm occupied Burnt Ash Farm in Baring Road, later the United Dairies, and had two local shops. One was at 168 Burnt Ash Hill, not far from Heather Road, and the other at 30 Burnt Ash Road – at the corner of Taunton Road, and now part of the Sainsbury site.

The Road to War

Fresh air was one of the principal remedies upon which the educational theorist Margaret McMillan relied in her efforts to improve the health and morale of the poor children of Deptford. As open space was not plentiful in the town she set up this 1912 camp in St Nicholas's graveyard. It may not be obvious from the equipment, but the boys were cooking pudding for their fellow campers' lunch.

A Greenwich tram swinging left past the White Hart at New Cross Gate and heading for Deptford along the New Cross Road, *c.* 1910.

At much the same time, a mile and a half to the south, these children were posed at a stile just off Crofton Park Road, opposite the end of Ewhurst Road. It gave access to a footpath that led across the fields, and along the garden wall of Brockley Hall, to the Brockley Jack pub. The footpath, which survived until the sale of the Brockley Hall estate in 1932, has now become the route of Sevenoaks Road.

The official group assembled to lay the foundation stone of New Cross Library on 6 September 1910, with the mayor and mayoress, Councillor and Mrs Berryman, in the centre. He is holding the silver trowel, and the town clerk, Vivian Orchard, has charge of the mace. It is sad to see that the dress sense of the Deptford councillor's wife was no more elevated than that of the East End costermonger's girl.

The London County Council, like Margaret McMillan, had great faith in open-air schools for the strengthening of children from deprived backgrounds. This weaving class was given in the grounds of Birley House, the council's open-air school in London Road, Forest Hill, now part of Horniman Gardens.

St Catherine's Church was built on the summit of Telegraph Hill in 1894, as an essential aid to the success of the Haberdashers' Company's smart new Hatcham estate. The photograph above shows it early in the twentieth century. In 1913 a mysterious fire – blamed upon the suffragettes – caused the damage shown below. St Catherine's has been unlucky. The repaired building was bombed in 1940 and not restored again until 1950.

The Lewisham Hippodrome in Rushey Green, the largest music hall in London, was opened in 1911. This must be a very early view, because it shows on the right the shop and garage that were demolished to make way for the Queen's Hall cinema, which opened in 1913.

The builder James Watt, one of the most influential figures in the development of Catford, was also a great provider of entertainment. He opened the Central Hall roller skating rink in Sangley Road in December 1908 and the Catford Picture Palace, two doors away, in April 1909. In January 1911 he was able to assemble this impressive group of employees of the twin establishments. It looks more like the general staff of the Ruritanian army.

These two views of the northern end of Lewisham High Street, *c.* 1910 and 1913, record a significant change. In the top picture, taken from the railway bridge, the plot next to St Stephen's Terrace, on the left, is occupied by the front office of Phil Ladd's nursery garden. It was one of many that flourished in Lewisham when it was a prosperous middle-class suburb, full of large houses and gardens. In 1912 it was replaced by the King's Hall cinema (below), a venture more profitably in tune with the taste of the area's new population.

With the country drifting towards war, the Lewisham Battalion of the National Reserve held a rally at the Catford-Southend Football Club ground in Mountsfield Park on the 6th of June 1914, before setting off on a fund-raising procession to Forest Hill. The members wore British army uniforms of all ages.

These NCOs were called back into service at the outbreak of the First World War to train the Lewisham Volunteers, who formed the second line of the Lewisham Gunners. They soon moved to the Ennersdale Road barracks at Hither Green, but this photograph is more likely to have been taken at the pre-war drill hall off Lewisham High Street, which stood between the Salisbury pub and the postal sorting office.

W.G. Grace, who was then living at Mottingham, near to the Army Service Corps HQ at Grove Park, did not at first think it right to play cricket during the war, but he relented in 1915 at the request of another former England captain, Archie MacLaren. MacLaren was serving with the ASC, and had decided to organise a charity match between the corps and Catford Cricket Club, in aid of Belgian refugees. The ASC side also included the great Jack Hobbs. The match took place on 23 of June, at Catford's ground in Penerley Road. Grace found himself too feeble to play, but he took round the collection boxes. It was to be his last recorded appearance on any cricket ground, and a few months later he was dead. The first six seated figures from the left in this group are Alec Hearne, the Kent professional, and one of a distinguished local cricketing family, Jack Hobbs, Horace French (the Catford captain), W.G. Grace, William Henry Le May, President of Catford CC (and Mayor of Lewisham in 1911/12), and Archie MacLaren.

Scouting was very popular during the First World War, when it gave boys a legitimate opportunity to put on uniforms and indulge in quasi-military exercises. This was the First Grove Park troop in 1917. They were attached to St Augustine's Church, but their hut stood nearly half a mile away, close to the Bromley border.

A train of horse artillery passing through Blackheath Village struggles up the steep hill of Lee Road to resume its march to the sea. This was a common sight here during the First World War, when troops often stopped to rest on the Heath.

The fund-raising floats that toured the streets of Deptford during the Red Cross Pageant of 20 October 1917 were filled with figures representing the various allied nations. The proceedings were professionally marshalled by G.Rhodes Parry, manager of the New Cross Empire. Here Brittania (impersonated by Miss Emmie Townson) is supported by Australia, South Africa, and India (Misses Florrie, Edie, and Amy Townson), and Canada (Miss Violet Bryer). Another attraction of the pageant was a Dutch auction conducted by Marie Lloyd.

The Bell Green gasworks, which employed the largest workforce in the Sydenham area, was hard pressed during both world wars, when the younger men were needed for the armed forces. Women were brought in to fill the gaps. Two are seen here working in the coal sheds in 1916.

King's biscuit factory in Staplehurst Road, next to Hither Green station, was also largely staffed by women during the First World War, when the firm was busy fulfilling contracts for the armed forces. This photograph was taken *c.* 1918.
The business was later renamed Chiltonian, and moved to new premises in Lee, seen on page 54.

Frederick Braby and Co., structural engineers and manufacturers of galvanised iron goods, had two large factories in Deptford, the Victoria Works between the Surrey Canal and Grove Street and the Ida Works between the canal and Deptford Park. When the Duke of York (later George VI) visited the Victoria Works in 1919 he apparently received a cool reception from at least part of the cloth-capped workforce.

The Changing
Twenties

Tea in the garden of The Pagoda, Blackheath's most exotic house, during the early 1920s. Frank Butcher of Butcher Curnow, the Tranquil Vale chemists and photographic dealers, then occupied The Pagoda, which had been built as a summerhouse in the middle of the eighteenth century.

Brockley Cemetery, although in Lewisham, was the property of Deptford Council, and it was here that the town's civilian victims of the Great War bombing raids were buried. Their memorial was unveiled by the mayor, Alderman Walter Green, on 24 July 1921, a day of glorious sunshine.

In the pioneering days of the railways an attempt was sometimes made to give dignity to the new technological wonder by basing the designs of the buildings on incongruous classical models. The staircase at Deptford Station on the London and Greenwich Railway was a case in point. The utilitarian twentieth century was not inclined to meet the repair bill for such extravagance and the staircase was demolished in 1927, a few years after this photograph was taken.

The photographer who recorded this early 1920s outing from the Brockley Jack would have been standing not far from the pub, but the charabanc was parked diagonally across the road outside the gates of Brockley Hall. This late survivor among the country houses of Lewisham was not demolished until 1932.

The London County Council's Bellingham Estate under construction in the early 1920s. The view is northwards from the Randlesdown Road area, and it is perhaps Brookehowse Road that is taking shape in the foreground. The words 'BUY' and 'GOLDEN' on the right are on the roof of Robertson's jam factory (demolished 1999) in Bromley Road.

Part of Lewisham High Street and
Hither Green, *c.* 1924. The main
feature in the High Street is the old
Lewisham Congregational church at
the corner of Courthill Road. At the
top of the picture the landmarks are
Hither Green station, at the junction
of the two lines, Leahurst Road School
to the left of the tracks, and the
parade ground of the Ennersdale Road
barracks to the right. The wooded
area on the right edge is the garden
of Campshill House in Hither Green
Lane. Near the bottom of the picture,
the triangle of lawn to the right of
the railway line is in the garden of the
Conservative Club, where the bowlers
(see pages 22–3) had been so busy a
quarter of a century before.

Each age provides its own appropriate background. Here are the dignified members of Lewisham Council, Victorians to a man (or, just occasionally, a woman) posed in 1924 in front of the dignified entrance to the old town hall. The mayor was then James Frederick Griffith. Fourth from the left in the second row is Alderman Furneaux, who can be seen with the Duke of York on page 56 during one of his own mayoral years.

New Cross Tram Depot in New Cross Road was the most important local battleground during the General Strike of May 1926. The photograph shows the scene outside, as large numbers of police, some mounted, cleared a way for the strike-breaking trams. The kerb is crowded with the cars of the middle-class heroes who helped to save the day.

The first stage in the construction of the London County Council's Downham Estate, in 1924. The photograph shows the builders' camp, with some of the earliest houses rising on the left. The view is eastwards towards Grove Park. The creation of Downham at the expense of Lewisham's last significant area of farmland was one of the major social and political events in the borough's history.

This photograph of the Downham Way end of Southover was taken in 1927, at the mid-point in the construction of the estate. Downham eventually added some forty thousand people, mostly from the slums of Deptford and Bermondsey, to the population of Lewisham.

Mrs Beatrice Drapper, who began her career as a gym mistress and swimming instructor in LCC schools, was the first woman to serve as mayor of Deptford, in 1927/8. Thankfull Sturdee's photograph shows the outgoing mayor, Alderman Hall, passing on the chain of office. Mrs Drapper later moved to Coniston Crescent, and was a Lewisham councillor from 1945 until 1958, but she failed to do the mayoral double. She died in 1961.

Students of the Clyde Street Men's Evening Institute at Deptford listening to a BBC broadcast on education for men, *c.* 1927. The home of the institute was the old Clyde Street School.

Mears Brothers making up Bellingham Road in 1928. It was only in that decade that the houses along this southern rampart of the Forster estate stretched out to meet those in Hazelbank Road, on the Corbett estate. Mears Brothers was a local firm, with works at 9 Weardale Road.

The Thames flood of 7 January 1928 created havoc in the Royal Victoria Victualling Yard at Deptford, hurling rum barrels in all directions and breaking down the yard's mighty walls. The photograph shows the early stages of the long process of clearing up and rebuilding.

In the years just before and after the First World War car repair workshops sprang up as rapidly as computer services in the '90s. This is Tooley's garage at no. 2a Burnt Ash Hill in the late 1920s. It occupied a tiny sliver of land to the south of the railway embankment, opposite Lee Station.

The Nervous Thirties

Refreshments on the way for some of the fairground workers running the
Blackheath Bank Holiday funfair in August 1931.

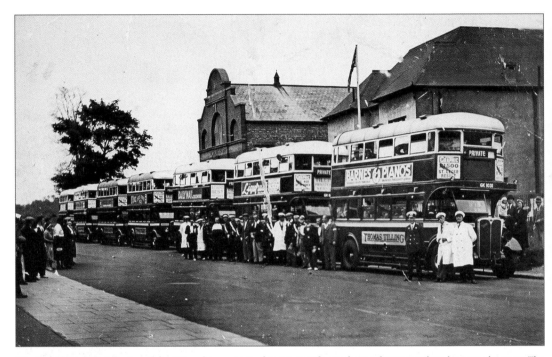

The flourishing British Legion Club at Downham organised many seaside coach trips for its members between the wars. The seven bus loads seen here, *c.* 1930, are about to depart from the club's premises in Old Bromley Road. The building beyond is the Salvation Army Hall.

An early 1930s staff outing from the Chiltonian biscuit factory in Manor Lane, Lee. The firm was previously known as King and Sons and located at Hither Green (see page 42). Its new model factory, now replaced by an industrial estate, was built between 1924 and 1930, when the whole operation was moved to Lee.

Another scene at the Blackheath Bank Holiday funfair of 4 August 1931 (see page 53). A worried London County Council had used its licensing powers to greatly reduce these events since the beginning of the century, but they were still much larger than any held on the Heath today.

Mill Road, Lewisham, seen through the Loampit Vale railway bridge in the early 1930s. Then the derelict Lewisham Bridge Mill still lay ahead of the girls, just around the corner, with the Maid of the Mill pub to its right. Now even the road has ceased to exist.

Rushey Green, opposite Catford Road, *c.* 1933. This stretch between Timpson's coach garage and C.A. Smallbone's off-licence has now been totally demolished. Some eighteenth-century houses, part of the old Rushey Green, were concealed behind the shopfronts.

The Duke of York, later King George VI, opened the Lewisham town hall extension, now the Lewisham Theatre and Town Hall Chambers, on 22 June 1932. He is seen here emerging from the building to a far more enthusiastic reception than he received at Deptford in 1919 (see page 42). With him is the mayor, Alderman Henry John Furneaux.

In the 1930s the government was anxious that local authorities should take advantage of slum clearance powers. The officials of Lewisham Council could find dull housing with their eyes shut, but slums were not so easy to locate. A few were identified, including Dacre Square, which lay on the south side of Dacre (later Fludyer) Street, in Lee New Town. It was demolished *c.* 1936, shortly after this photograph was taken.

One of the most contentious local issues of the 1920s, '30s, and '40s was the Downham Wall, a barricade raised by the middle class residents of Alexandra Crescent in 1926 to maintain their separation from the hoi polloi on the London County Council's new Downham estate. The LCC had thought to make this one of the estate's main road links with Bromley. Persuasion failed to secure the wall's removal for nearly twenty-five years, and it was not until 1950 that Bromley Council consigned it to the history of class warfare.

Was there ever a time and place when plus fours were *de rigueur* for crazy golf? At Catford, apparently, in the 1930s, when this course was established next to St Laurence's church, on what is now part of the site of Laurence House. The western end of the old town hall can be seen in the background, on the other side of Catford Road.

59

During the Munich crisis of 1938 many councils acted on Home Office advice by taking air raid precautions. Among emergency measures in Lewisham during the September of that year were the protection of the town hall with sandbags – the entrance to the concert hall section, photographed in happier days on page 56, is shown below – and the digging of trenches in Rushey Green (above) and elsewhere in the borough. The firm that secured this contract was soon paid to level most of the trenches again, but these ones in Rushey Green were made permanent in June 1939.

In defiance of international despondancy the management of Cobb's department store at Sydenham spent the late 1930s rebuilding much of the shop. In June 1939 Graham Moffatt, the cheeky fat boy in Will Hay's classic films, was invited to preside over the opening festivities. He is seen here preparing to pull the string that will smash a bottle of champagne on the dome. Just over a year later most of the modernised building was a bomb site.

Immediately on the outbreak of war the nurses of St John's hospital, Morden Hill, were evacuated to Aylesford in Kent. They are seen here in September 1939 at the café on the Maidstone Road that was requisitioned as their canteen.

Deptford's flamboyant town hall, which had been opened with such pride in 1905 (see page 24), was one of the borough's most precious assets, and great trouble was taken to protect it as soon as war was declared. This was all the more important as the building was also the local civil defence headquarters. The photograph was taken in September 1939.

War and
Reconstruction

Thirty-eight pupils and six teachers were killed on the spot, and many others seriously injured at Sandhurst Road School on 20 January 1943. The building had been cut in half by a bomb dropped by a low-flying raider. Normal reporting restrictions were lifted to exploit the propaganda possibilities of this daylight attack on children. In the foreground of the picture is a Salvation Army canteen set up for the rescue services.

The Park (later Hither Green) Fever Hospital was badly damaged by bombing on the night of 11 September 1940. A stoker named John Foley won the George Medal for rescuing a nurse from the burning staff sick quarters during this raid.

The men and women of Lewisham Wardens' Post G108 photographed outside their headquarters in 1940 or 1941. The post, which could hardly have accommodated all of them simultaneously, was in Blythe Hill Lane, at the bottom of the garden of 34 Ravensbourne Road.

Even the passages of history that flash by with the most breathless speed on the page can seem wearyingly slow to those who live through them. The jobs of air raid wardens and rescue squads could sometimes be very tedious, and the provision of simple entertainments was soon found to be essential. These draughts players were at the Woodyates Road depot near Lee station, formerly a Lewisham council yard. The darts match was photographed at the Malpas Road depot, the chief civil defence post for southern Deptford. The photographs were taken in 1940 and 1941.

The tiresome modern craze for weeks and months and years devoted to some cause or movement perhaps had its origin during the war, when such occasions were frequently used for fund raising or propaganda. The function of Deptford Youth Week in October 1942 was to enrol children in clubs and other organisations and to discourage them from sabotaging emergency water tanks. The children's canteen, seen here at the junction of Upper Brockley Road and Lewisham Way during one of the week's parades, was a gift from Australia.

Bethray's bakery at 2 Woodpecker Road, Deptford, at the corner of Edward Street, being demolished in June 1942, after serious bomb damage. A barrage balloon makes a vain gesture of defence.

The end of a home. This couple were lucky to escape with their lives when Etta Street in Deptford was bombed on 20 January 1943. Two people were killed. This was the fighter-bomber raid in which Sandhurst Road School was hit (see page 63).

During that same surprise attack on 20 January 1943 eleven people died when nos 5 and 7 Oscar Street in Deptford New Town suffered a direct hit. In all, 107 people were killed during this eighty-eight plane raid. Only three fighter-bombers and six escort fighters were shot down.

Bored children getting up to mischief were a problem during the war. One solution thought of by the Deptford Beautification and Social Amenities Committee, as part of its Holidays at Home campaign, was a day of women's and children's sports at the New Cross Stadium on 29 July 1943. This merry-go-round was a big attraction. Second prize in the fancy dress competition was won with a flame-coloured creation entitled 'Midnight in Hamburg'!

One of the best-known buildings lost to the V1 flying bombs was Forest Hill station, which was so seriously damaged on 23 June 1944 that it was never fully repaired, although the shell stood for decades after the war. The bomb, which landed on the pedestrian subway, totally destroyed W.H. Smith's and Chalk and Cox's butchers

Lewisham was the only local hospital to receive a direct hit by a flying bomb. It fell on 26 July 1944, destroying two wards and the registrar's office, and causing extensive damage to the whole complex. The photograph was taken in September 1944. It was only in the 1950s that the hospital began to recover its pre-war capacity.

The most deadly of all the V2 rocket attacks on Britain between September 1944 and March 1945 devastated New Cross Road on 25 November. It totally destroyed a crowded branch of Woolworths and seriously damaged the Royal Arsenal Co-Op next door. The casualties were 168 killed and 123 seriously injured. The photograph shows the view across the cleared site of Woolworths towards the scarred Deptford Town Hall.

VE (Victory in Europe) Day was celebrated with street parties all over the country on 8 May 1945. The precedent had been set in peace time, to mark various coronations and royal jubilees. This example of the familiar scene was in Taunton Road, Lee.

Queen Mary opened the
Stanstead Lodge Darby and
Joan club at Forest Hill
on 30 April 1949. In this
group she is flanked by
Herbert Morrison, MP for
East Lewisham, and Mrs
Morrison, and by Alderman
John Thomas Cummings,
the Mayor of Lewisham,
and Mrs Cummings. The
club was a project the
eighty-four-year-old Mayor
had very much at heart,
and completed just before
the end of his term of
office.

The winter and spring of 1948/9 was a busy time for Herbert Morrison, who was then Lord President of the Council. On 2 December he was in Hither Green Lane to open the first block of Lewisham's Hether Grove Estate. The photograph shows his official and unofficial audiences on either side of the fence. On 11 March it was the turn of Morse House, the first block completed on the Flower House estate at Southend. He is seen on the left conducting the Jones family into flat four. Fifty years on, the experimental blocks on these two estates, 'constructed for speed', have been replaced by houses.

The Still Point

The bone-shaking trams were not necessarilly popular favourites during most of their reign on the London streets but, in the early 1950s, the news that they were to be scrapped provoked a surge of sentimental affection. This interior view of a upper saloon shows how well they were patronised during that period.

Although the national Labour vote at the 1950 general election was well down from its landslide levels of 1945, and the party barely retained a majority, Jack Cooper romped home in the Deptford constituency with a majority of nearly fifteen thousand. He is standing second from the right in this group of Deptford worthies. The others are, left to right, the mayor, E.A. Robinson, W.J. Stimpson, JP, and Ernest Field, the town clerk, who should perhaps have been tempering his smile with a neutral frown.

London said a long, but apparently not a final, farewell to the trams on 5 July 1952, when the last six routes were surrendered to the buses. It was an emotional week for devotees, but here at the clock tower their passing was just an opportunity for graffiti. The last runs were like the end of a Will Hay or Marx Brothers film, as souvenir hunting passengers stripped the cars of everything detachable.

In February 1953, when the BBC's *Workers' Playtime* was broadcast from the Gleniffer Laundry in Bromley Road for the third time, the featured entertainers included Alfred Marks and the 'up and coming young script-writer' Bob Monkhouse. They are seen here with the producer Bill Gates, singers Barbara Leigh and Lee Lawrence, and some of the four hundred laundresses.

A religious service in a greyhound stadium must be an uncommon event. One took place at Catford on 31 May 1953, in response to the Queen's request that her people should pray for her on the eve of her coronation. More than five thousand people attended the United Service of Dedication organised by the Vicar of Lewisham, Canon P.D. Robb.

The Queen and Prince Philip made several tours through the London boroughs in the week after the coronation. Lewisham's turn came on 8 June 1953, when the royal car drove along Brockley Road, Adelaide Avenue, Ladywell Road, Lewisham High Street, Rushey Green, and Brownhill Road. It is seen here turning from Ladywell Road into the High Street, past the bomb site now occupied by the Ladywell Leisure Centre.

What was reported as probably the first ever Hindu wedding service in Lewisham was celebrated at 91 Belmont Hill on 4 April 1953. That was the home of the groom, Om Prakash Agrawai, a company director, because the bride, Janak Dulari, lived in a flat. Her father worked at India House, and guests included the High Commissioner and many diplomats.

Another exotic scene. St John's Presbyterian church in Devonshire Road has long been the centre of Scottish expatriate life in Forest Hill. At this Burns night supper in 1953 (held in what was then the hall, now the church) the haggis is seen being piped around the table, a tradition that must prevent its ever being served piping hot.

Not quite the shape of things to come. In August 1954 J.C. Pendleton, Senior Assistant to the Borough Architect, explains the plans for the rebuilding of Lewisham town hall to the mayor, Councillor Braithwaite. Is he saying 'We can always get rid of the clock tower at a later stage'? John Penn, who had known Lewisham when the old town hall was the very latest thing, looks on disdainfully from his plinth.

The Towell family of 101 Algernon Road, Lewisham, packing for their annual hop-picking holiday at Chilham, near Canterbury, in August 1954. This was almost the end of an old tradition. The mechanisation of the larger farms, the introduction of paid holidays in factories, and the disapproval of the school authorities, had all been factors contributing to a sharp decline in the numbers making the pilgrimage to Kent.

The Cooper twins, Henry and George, Bellingham's favourite sons, signed professional contracts with Jim Wicks in July 1954, as the highlight of the BBC's *Sportsview* programme. The commentators Peter Dimmock and Harry Carpenter acted as witnesses. The agreements must have been post-dated, as the boxers had a previous engagement with Her Majesty's government, to complete their national service. Both were in the Army.

In October 1954 an attempt was made to reverse a decline in Civil Defence recruitment with the aid of exhibitions and parades. This fifty-vehicle procession passed through the borough on 2 October and, at the town hall in Catford Road, the mayor and other Lewisham dignitaries were on the saluting platform to greet it.

Television cameras rolled for the first time at Downham Baths on 14 and 15 January 1955, when London had an easy victory over Berlin in the annual inter-city swimming match.

Lewisham's bemused housewives got their first taste of supermarket shopping on 20 September 1955, when the new Sainsbury's branch, then the largest self-service food store in the country, opened its doors. Alan Sainsbury was there to welcome the first customers, and there was even an explanatory strip-cartoon in the local paper. The building, no. 132 Lewisham High Street, was replaced in the 1970s by the main entrance of the Lewisham Centre and the shops on the north side of the mall.

These late eighteenth-century buildings in Tranquil Vale have seen many strange sights, no doubt – see page 40, for an example – but it seems unlikely that any camels had passed them before October 1955. These alleged Foreign Legion veterans from Algeria were the stars of Billy Smart's circus, then appearing on Blackheath.

When the Savoy Rooms at 75 Rushey Green opened in March 1955, 800 people were admitted and 400 disappointed dancers were turned away. (The hilarity of the fortunate revellers was enhanced by their knowledge that this had until recently been the local food office, the scene of endless queuing for ration books.) By October 1957, when this photograph was taken, the management was resorting to bizarre stunts to draw the crowds. 'Mackeson Night', with cash prizes for superior silliness, was the latest Wednesday attraction.

The most serious train crash on the Southern Region, and the third worst in British railway history, took place between St John's and Lewisham stations on 4 December 1957, when a Ramsgate express ploughed into the back of a Hayes suburban service, causing the flyover above the trains to collapse. Ninety people were killed and one hundred and nine seriously injured. Rescue efforts were hampered by the fog that helped to cause the accident.

On the night of the 3/4 of January 1958 a host of stage and screen stars came to the Lewisham Gaumont (later the Odeon) to take part in a 'midnight matinée' in aid of the mayor's relief fund for the victims of the crash. Those taking part included Richard Attenborough, Ian Carmichael, Vera Lynn, Dorothy Squires, Petula Clark, and the boxer Freddie Mills. Here are Frankie Howerd and Joan Sims at the stage door.

The Prime Minister, Harold
Macmillan, speaking outside
St Stephen's church in
Lewisham High Street on
3 October 1959, while
the newsreel cameras roll.
Supermac was supporting
Christopher Chataway, the
Conservative candidate
for Lewisham North, who
stands behind his leader with
modestly bowed head. The
general election was held on
8 October. In this greatly
changed section of the High
Street notice particularly the
Victorian Roebuck, on the left,
which was soon to be replaced
by the present building in
Rennell Street.

87

Christopher Chataway, who had made his name as an athlete, canvassing in Lewisham during the 1959 campaign, the first in which the local black vote was a factor the politicians took seriously. Chataway won his election and represented Lewisham North until 1966.

Watch it Come Down

The second stage of the town hall rebuilding plan outlined in 1954 (see page 81) involved the demolition, early in 1961, of the shops known as the Catford Arcade. They had been built in the 1928 on the site of Hatcliffe's Almshouses, at the junction of Catford Road and Catford Broadway.

A 1930s investigation found that
some of the worst of the few slums in
the Lewisham area were at Bell Green,
Sydenham. It would eventually have
been necessary to clear them all had
not the Luftwaffe done much of the
work while aiming at the gas works.
This view, probably taken from the
roof of the old Sydenham Brewery
in Porthcawe Road in January 1961,
shows the parts of Bell Green Lane
(on the left) and Relinque, Porthcawe,
and Maddin Roads that had been
occupied by prefabs since the war.
They had now been cleared, and the
surviving Victorian terraces were
about to be demolished, as the council
prepared to build the tower blocks
that now cover the site. The huge
Brittanic House Club is the landmark
on the left.

91

The town clerk's general office, otherwise known as the typing pool, at Lewisham town hall in April 1961. The clerks from 50 Tanner's Hill (see page 21) might not have felt too out of place here. Now, in less than forty years, it has become almost as remote as the office in *A Christmas Carol*.

Also from April 1961 comes this scene of trading standards officers (or is it public health inspectors?) spoiling the day of a Lewisham grocer. But where was this well-stocked and stylishly furnished shop?

The Surrey Canal was one of the main arteries for Deptford's trade throughout the nineteenth century and during the first half of the twentieth. It was still fairly well used, especially as a centre for saw-milling, when this photograph was taken in 1962, but the decline had already begun and soon became rapid. The canal closed in the '70s.

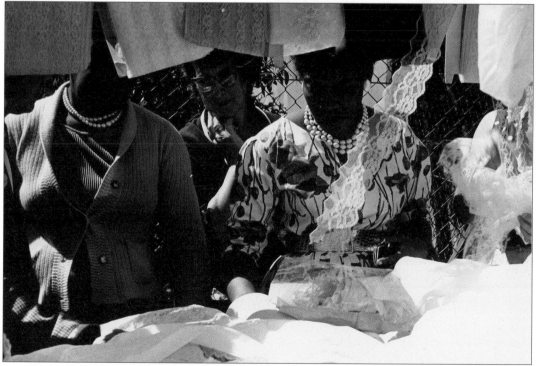

A 1962 scene in Deptford Market, which continues to be a lively feature of life in the town nearly forty years later.

Tommy Steele lived for a time in Ravensbourne Park and was hailed in 1957 as 'Catford's Own Rock and Roll King'. He is seen here at Sydenham County School, Dartmouth Road, in November 1963. His sister attended the school and persuaded Tommy to open a fair, and witness her perfomance in a scene from *Half a Sixpence*. He could not resist reclaiming his own famous role.

When the Beatles played the Lewisham Odeon in March 1963 they were third on the bill behind two forgotten American singers. They returned triumphantly six months later to a cinema besieged for days by teenagers desperate for tickets. One of the few to notice them during their first visit was local journalist Paula Gracey, who was rewarded with a second interview – and a sweet – on stage at the Odeon on 7 December 1963. In March she was sporting Audrey Hepburn hair but now the style was veering towards Cilla Black.

The Lewisham seats were important marginals during the 1964 general election campaign and both party leaders visited the borough. Sir Alec Douglas Hume, the Prime Minister, spoke in Sydenham and in Lewisham High Street on 3 July. This was the scene in the Greyhound car park, where the trains pulling into Sydenham station must have hindered the oratorical flow.

Harold Wilson, the Leader of the Opposition, drew a larger crowd in the playground of St Mary's Schools in Lewisham High Street on 19 September. What would the conservative founders of the National Schools have thought of a socialist speaking there? Wilson's winning slogan at the election (proving that there is nothing new under the sun) was 'For a New Britain'.

95

The most prominent landmarks of domestic brutalism in the centre of the borough are the three tower blocks on the High Street side of Lewisham Park. I have not been able to trace an architect anxious to claim the credit but the structural engineer was S.M. Cleator. The photograph shows one of the blocks, probably Bredgar, being built in 1964. Until that decade the open space had been a private pleasure ground for the residents of the surrounding houses.

The smiling strength of the Deptford Meals on Wheels service posed in 1965, just before the borough ceased to exist, on amalgamation with Lewisham. The photograph was taken in the council's Giffin Street depot.

Until the 1860s Lee Green Farm stood here at the corner of Burnt Ash Road and Eltham Road. The shops that replaced it must have been a startling change for the rural Victorian population of the village. What would they have thought of Leegate House and the Leegate shopping centre, for which the shops were demolished a century later, in 1967? On its day this is now the windiest and most desolate spot in all Lewisham.

The junction of Lewisham High Street and Loampit Vale, known as the Obelisk, was usually a difficult one for motorists (see page 103), but it was rarely as bad as this. The Ravensbourne and Quaggy, which converge just to the north of this spot, and the Ravensbourne's other main tributary, the Pool, have all had a long history of overflowing, and there were several floods in the 1960s. The Greater London Council responded with an expensive three-year programme of preventative measures, but the works were still a few weeks short of completion when two days of storms caused the rivers to break their banks in spectacular style on 16 September 1968.

On the March

The view up Tanners Hill in the early 1970s. The new flats on the west side were then still confronted by one of the doomed terraces of Deptford New Town, which had not really been new for 150 years. The menacing object in the background is Pitman House.

This fine view of Deptford in transition was taken in the early 1970s, probably from Camellia House in Idonia Street. The totally demolished road on the left is Octavius Street. The partially demolished Douglas Way, with its market in full swing, fills most of the picture, and leads the eye to Deptford High Street. Prominent landmarks in the background include the soap factory chimney in Frankham Street and, on the right, Mumford's Mill on Deptford Creek.

The Riverdale Mill at
Lewisham, in which the
great John Penn (see page
81) spent his early years,
was used as a bakery
by John Wallis Ltd. for
the first seventy years of
the century. Most of the
complex, including the
buildings seen here
c. 1970, were swept
away soon afterwards
as part of the Lewisham
Centre/Molesworth Street
development, and the
Riverdale offices now cover
much of the site. The oldest
mill building survives in
Moleworth Street.

Which Lewisham Road has been changed the most in the last thirty years, without being entirely abolished? Not the High
Street, as one might at first think. Not even Deptford Church Street, a more considered second choice. It is surely Molesworth
Street, which is seen here *c.* 1970. The view is northwards towards the Odeon cinema.

Rush-hour traffic at the Obelisk junction (see pages 86–7, 98, and 114) in the early 1970s. All the buildings visible here have been demolished during the 1990s, and the great northern roundabout of Lewisham High Street now occupies the whole area.

A scene in Deptford High Street during the 1970s. No. 61 was the Rossi Brothers' café until the early '70s, and became a jewellery shop in the early '80s. The shrimps and winkles presumably filled the vacancy.

This photograph of the construction of the Evelyn Estate at Deptford, taken *c.* 1970, might be regarded as a representative image for the decade that had just ended. What mind could take pleasure in conceiving such a domestic environment – for other people? And who had the idea of naming the monstrosity after a gardener and lover of forest trees?

The first phase of the Lewisham Centre, towards Molesworth Street, was opened in October 1975, and the second, including the main High Street entrance (seen here), in November 1976; but it was evidently still incomplete when this photograph was taken six months later. The building of this large shopping precinct during the middle years of the decade transformed the appearance of the High Street, led directly to the closure of Lewisham's only department store (see page 108), and set the scene for the even greater changes of the 1990s.

The crazy politics of the 1970s hit the streets of Lewisham on 13 August 1977, when extremists of the right and left clashed violently while the decent people of the borough looked on in horror. A National Front march from New Cross to Lewisham was confronted by the Socialist Workers' Party and other groups. The photograph shows a National Front man being attacked in New Cross Road. The police, struggling to keep the factions apart, took most of the casualties.

Brilliant research by Peter Guillery has recently established that no. 150 Deptford High Street, seen here in 1977, is a late seventeenth-century house of great architectural interest, and one of the oldest buildings in the borough. In the 1990s the bomb site on the left was filled with a shop designed in close imitation of the style of its neighbour.

Stormy Weather

The splendid Deptford Odeon, which had been opened with such high hopes in 1938, had the longest and least dignified death of any local cinema. It was closed in 1970, ten years before this photograph was taken, and was not finally demolished until 1988. During those eighteen years countless plans and proposals came and went, while the building became a more and more disgraceful eyesore.

In 1980, in a forlorn bid for survival, the management of Chiesman's department store persuaded the council to permit the building of this bizarre footbridge across the High Street, to link it with the Lewisham Shopping Centre. It is seen here in 1982. Few were persuaded to use it, except as a curiosity. For the fate of the bridge see page 118 and the back endpaper.

When the Lewisham Brewery was built in 1817 it dominated the village like a great white palace rising at the bend of the Ravensbourne valley. Over a century and three quarters it crumbled and dwindled, as the brewing of beer was moved away and the premises were used by Whitbread & Co. only as a bottling plant. The end came in 1985, when the whole complex except the office on Lewisham Road (now Eagle House) was demolished to make way for the Tesco supermarket.

The airship and aircraft designer Sir Barnes Wallis, most famous for his dambusting bouncing bombs, lived at no. 241 New Cross Road between 1891 and 1915. A commemorative plaque was unveiled at the house on 29 of September 1984 by Sir Barnes' sister, Mrs Annie Knight, who is seated in the foreground. The inventor's son and daughter were also present.

In 1986 the Thames at Deptford, seen here from the Pepys Estate, was still apparently a busy commercial river, but industry had already been in retreat for many years. The process has accelerated since then, and now even the landmark power station has gone. The Japanese ship is alongside the Convoy's newsprint wharf.

The Great Storm that swept over England on 15 and 16 October 1987 killed eighteen people, damaged practically every building in its path and uprooted fifteen million trees. It seemed at the time that the country must be permanently scarred, but soon nature recovered and the changes ceased to be noticed. Lewisham's experience of the storm was no different in kind from that of a thousand other places, but some record of the dramatic event must be included here. The night gave a wonderful boost to the motor industry, as thousands of vehicles shared the fate of the Granville Park car above. In Eliot Park the road entirely disappeared beneath a carpet of branches and leaves.

Walter Segal, the German architect who settled in England in 1936, devised a style of timber-framed houses that the intended occupants could largely build for themselves, refining the details to their own requirements. Lewisham was the only council willing to try the experiment, beginning in 1978. Segal Close, off Brockley Park, Forest Hill, (completed in 1981), was named in honour of the pioneer, who died four years later. The photograph shows the new street in the late '80s.

The closure and almost complete demolition of St John's Hospital, and the intensive redevelopment of the site, provoked some controversy in the 1980s. The most widely regretted hospital building was the 1938 nurses' home on Lewisham Hill, designed by Bertram Carter, and much admired by those who admire that kind of thing. It is the heap of rubble on the right of this 1989 view. The photograph also shows the beginnings of some of the tiny houses that have replaced it.

Brave New World

The Lewisham Odeon met its unmaker in 1991, after lying empty for a full decade. It had been opened almost sixty years before, in 1932, as the Gaumont, and in its day had been one of the great cinemas and concert venues of London. (See pages 85 and 94.) The photographer, Stephen Moreton Prichard, calls his picture *The Twilight of the Gods*.

Young Lewisham observes the passing of the old in 1991. The Victorian Lewisham Bridge on which the boys were standing was soon to vanish, like so much else that they will not remember.

The drinkers of the Loampit Vale area have suffered from the changes of the 1990s, with the recent loss of the fine Mid Kent Tavern to the Docklands Light Railway station and, earlier, the demolition of the Duke of Cambridge, to make way for the Obelisk roundabout. Here is a farewell glimpse of the boarded-up Duke in January 1992. All the shops in the picture have also been swept away.

Like a Cunard liner run
aground in Catford Road,
Laurence House, the
Lewisham town hall annex,
looms against the May sky in
1992. St Laurence's church
was demolished in 1968 to
make way for the extension,
but the site remained an
untidy car park for twenty-
two years before this bulky
anticlimax was built.

Did anyone collect statistics for traffic accidents in the vicinity before, during, and after the mercifully brief appearance of
these Sumo wrestlers in Lewisham High Street? They are seen here in October 1993, on the roundabout at the southern end
of Molesworth Street. It is now occupied by another work of art.

Amid all the changes in
Lewisham it is good to see
that something remains
the same. It is 1995, and
St Stephen's church looks
out serenely on the Obelisk
junction as it has done for
130 years, although there
are few buildings left that it
knew in its youth.

After the closure and demolition of the Army and Navy department store (formerly Chiesman's) it was possible in 1995 to remove the unsightly footbridge across the High Street (see page 108). The photograph shows it being hauled northwards towards the Obelisk roundabout. (The man was not wielding a whip, but a telephone.) Yet Lewisham has still not rid itself of the bridge. Its latest resting place is seen on the back endpaper.

Not even the clock tower, the most familiar landmark of the borough, was immune from the Lewisham 2000 changes of the 1990s. In 1995, just before its centenary, the tower was dismantled and re-erected some ten yards to the west, out of the way of the traffic. The opportunity was taken to clean the stonework and retouch the gilding of the crown. The photograph shows the removal of the clock, the original mechanism of which has been donated to the National Museum of Science and Industry.

The Lewisham Model Market in the High Street, which scarcely seems the model for anything at all, is seen here in 1997. It was apparently opened in the 1930s, and by the '50s dealt mainly in food, fancy goods, and antiques. It is now very miscellaneous, with a bias towards clothing.

Old Lewisham resident Spike Milligan returned on 26 November 1998 to cut the ribbon before two new historical murals in the Lewisham Centre. He is seen here signing autographs after the ceremony. Spike told one fan that he was determined to outlive Harry Secombe, for fear the blighter should sing at his funeral.

The century ends with the demolition of St George's, Woolstone Road, one of the most distinctive of the borough's Victorian churches. Sadly, it appears to have been built upon sand, or possibly clay. The melancholy work is seen in progress in July 1999.

Acknowledgements & Picture Credits

For their generous assistance I have to thank Mr Dennis Adams, Mrs C. Cooper, Mr Ken George, Mr A. Hackman, Mr Stephen Moreton Prichard, Mrs Eileen Simmons, Mr John West, and Mr Gus White.

Most of the photographs are from the Lewisham Local Studies Centre, and are reproduced by kind permission of the London Borough of Lewisham. Others are the property of the author, or are from originals belonging to:

Stephen Moreton Prichard: pages 103, bottom; 105, top; 107; 108, both; 110; 111, both; 112, bottom; 113; 114, both; 115, bottom; 116–17; 118, top; 119; 120, bottom; back endpaper

A. Hackman: pages 25, top; 28, both; 32, both; 35, top; 36, top

London Metropolitan Archives: page 45, bottom; 49, both

John West: pages 14; 72–3

Gus White: page 35, bottom

Catford Cyphers Cricket Club: pages 38–9

Mrs C. Cooper: page 43

Mrs Eileen Simmons: page 64, bottom